Wealth Within Reach

Wealth Within Reach, Volume 1

George M Potter

Published by Tin Bucket Media, LLC., 2023.

WEALTH WITHIN REACH

First edition. April 3, 2023.

ISBN: 979-8215885468

Written by George M Potter.

Table of Contents

Preface

Some things you need to know before you begin.

I am extremely happy that you have opened this book.

As you read, you will understand why I'm happy that you have done so. You are giving me the opportunity to pass on the expertise I've earned over a lifetime and will share with you. This expertise will provide you with the framework to build your own wealth from this moment onward.

It's not only about money. But it's not about money either. . .

My background in this field – Personal Finance, Investing, Financial Planning, or whatever updated terms you wish to use – covers nearly my entire life.

When I was 5 years old, I learned about interest rates. At 9 years old, I learned what owning company stock really meant and how stockbrokers earned a living. At 12, all on my own, I opened my first passbook savings account and brought my jar from home, stuffed with coins and $1 bills I had earned doing chores for my parents.

I learned these things, how they worked, and what they could do for me, from a father who was a financial advisor, stockbroker, and consultant to venture capitalists. This is what he taught me. What you are about to read in this book, and the books in this series, is our legacy.

Many years later, and while my father was still alive, I pursued and found a position as a financial advisor at American Express Financial Advisors – later to be renamed Ameriprise Financial. I started there in the year 2000. Historically, it was the last year of the technology boom and my office was right in the center of Silicon Valley. Nearly all of my clients worked in the high-tech field. The first few years were, as expected, difficult and I nearly lost my position as a Financial Advisor when the tech crash began during my first year.

A few years later, as luck would have it, another crash appeared on the horizon.

In early 2008, I experienced a moment of clarity. I was alone and sitting at my desk in an office on the 8th floor. My window looked out at the sprawl of Silicon Valley and at the eight lanes of highway traffic below. I remember the moment when I saw what the next few years would bring. There were too many financial indicators telling me the housing market and the attached financial instruments were about to go bust.

I also saw clearly how this bust was going to impact me and the business I had worked so hard to develop.

I knew it was coming and I began to advise my clients to step away from the stock and mutual fund markets for the foreseeable future. Nearly every one of them took my advice on faith after working together for several years. Two of them did not and they paid dearly for this decision.

As a result, clients who were planning to send their children to college were able to do that. Clients who were working to pay off their mortgage early were able to do that. Clients who were near their retirement were able to do that too, even though the financial markets were crumbling around them. For many years afterward, I received annual Christmas cards from dozens of them out of appreciation.

Unfortunately, I eventually had to sell the equity in my practice and I left Ameriprise Financial in early 2009. Because nearly all of my clients who had retreated from the stock market because of my recommendation, and because my revenue was based on fees for managing their assets, I could no longer sustain any of the expenses associated with a professional practice.

Were it not for the financial collapse, I would still be advising this same group of people, and hopefully a few more.

You need to understand the source of the information you are about to be exposed to in the first book of the Wealth Within Reach series. I am not some internet guru nor a guru in any sense of the word. I am not building a personal brand nor am I trying to gain a legion of followers. I am simply trying to reach out and help as many people as I can with what I know. This was the basis of my financial planning business and it is the basis of the book you are about to read.

At Ameriprise Financial, there was a Mission Statement printed and on display in the lobby at our offices nationwide. The most important part of that Mission Statement was "the client comes first." I took this to heart in everything I did.

In this book, "the reader comes first" and you will find many helpful passages that describe strategies or tactics that are based on what you need to hear. You will not find any passage in this book that is not focused on this one idea.

For your protection, you will find a disclaimer at the end of every part of this book. My intention is not to scare you but to remind you constantly, for your protection, that the responsibility for what you do with your money is yours alone.

If, however, you are reading this book with the intention of taking charge of your finances then I welcome you, encourage you, and applaud you. Your desire to finally understand how to save, invest, budget, and plan is something everyone should pursue.

After all, it's your money. Whether you have large sums or small, you need to pay attention to it.

It is your responsibility to understand how to manage your money. The responsibility is not mine nor is it anyone else's. The financial institutions you choose to do business with or the financial products you choose to purchase are solely at your discretion. You will not find any recommendations in these books as to which financial firm to use or where you should buy any financial products you might be considering.

This is a How-To book. This book is about managing the money you already have.

What you will find in the books of this series are practical and usable techniques and strategies to build financial wealth. There are no magic formulas. There are no secret skills. Anybody can build wealth. Financial wealth is, fundamentally, one of the easiest things to build but most people simply don't know where to start.

I welcome you and hope to see you on the last page.

If you have not done so already . . .

Please join us on our website – tinbucketfinance.com. I publish weekly blog posts about various personal finance topics and will notify you by email about new posts. This blog is free simply because "The Reader Comes First."

> **Disclaimer:** Any financial advice, technique, or opportunity revealed in this series of books or anything pertaining to financial markets, in part or as a whole, is purely for informational purposes only.

Introduction

This is what you will find in Book #1

Let's begin at the Beginning.

Welcome to the first book in our series. In the pages of this book, we will begin at the beginning and proceed to build the foundations of wealth.

If you are in your 20's and just starting out, or if you are in your 60's and making a move to retire soon, you will find financial information here that will surprise, engage, and encourage you to build your desired level of wealth and, most importantly, how to keep it. For everyone, starting at the beginning is often the most important step. For some, returning to the beginning will erase many mistakes.

No matter where you are on the financial journey, *Wealth Within Reach: Book 1*, will indeed be worthwhile to read. Use the information you find here to build the strongest foundation possible. It is after all, what will ultimately support your financial house for the rest of your life.

In the following pages, I will show you the 4 key areas that support wealth building. No matter whether you wish to become a billionaire or simply "well-off" in the future, these four key areas are necessary. No one has ever built wealth without them.

I can imagine every kind of reader while I write this book. Some are wealthy already. Some have worked most of their adult lives with little to show for it. Others are making a good living in their chosen careers and want to get "serious." There may even be readers who are just starting out in their professional lives and want to get "serious" about their money ahead of time. There are single mothers who are getting frustrated. There are couples who want to raise a family but don't think it is possible. There are men and women who have worked all their lives and want to retire soon, but don't know if they can.

In each and every case, they have created a vision for what they want even if they don't see how to get there. You are no exception to this process. Hold onto that image. Refer to it often. This is what will help you when you reach difficult periods in your life and what you will celebrate when the going is easy.

I can offer the suggestion of writing down your goals so that you are clear about what you want. I can do that. However, I have a better way for you. It is a more thorough way and one way to provide you with the best chance of seeing this vision come to life.

A number of years ago, I read a very simple book. It was written many decades ago and the language is dated and, initially, difficult to read. I progressed through it and when I reached the end, I realized that the short-term effort I put into reading this famous book was worth every minute.

If you want a better financial life, or simply a better life in general, I recommend that you read *Think and Grow Rich*, by Napoleon Hill. While the book you are reading right now is about practical steps, *Think and Grow Rich* is about a higher-level mindset that will broaden your perspective about wealth and how to receive it. Napoleon Hill's book has been in print for so long that copies can be found dirt cheap. Look it up on Amazon.com. You will not be wasting your time if you read it cover to cover.

Let's begin with a thought experiment.

No matter who you are or how wealthy you believe yourself to be, I want you to imagine something. I want you to fully imagine yourself in a life where all of your income goes to you. You don't have any bills. There is nothing withheld from your paycheck. All the things in life that are necessities are provided to you at no expense. Every single penny of your income is yours to do with as you wish.

How does that feel?

Do you feel wealthy? You should.

Are you motivated to increase your wealth or are you satisfied with this level of abundance? There is no wrong answer to this question.

In the first section of this book, I am going to show you how to determine where all your income goes each month. You may already have a good idea, but we are going to take it further and find out where every single penny goes. This is the first step of building wealth. Call it "Taking Stock" if you wish, but when you understand where it all goes, you have created the basis for deciding where it will go in the future and *where it shouldn't.*

If you could eliminate or reduce some of your expenses, you would be closer to realizing the dream from the thought experiment. You may not reach the point where all your expenses are paid for from a source other than your income, but you will see the value of your greatest asset. Your income (from employment or your investments) is the asset that will foster, discover, and develop your ability to accumulate wealth for the rest of your life.

Reducing your expenses and increasing your income are the two forces we will deal with in Book #1. So, grab a pad of paper, a pen or pencil, and let's begin your journey.

<u>Special Note to the Reader</u>: I sincerely hope that you did not skip over the preface to this book. There, if you remember, is a brief description of my history and expertise. In the following pages, every word I write in this book is written as if you were a client of mine. I was genuinely interested in the lives of all my clients when I was a financial advisor and now, I am interested in the lives of my readers. Understand this as you go along. Understand that I hope what you hope. I dream for you the same things you dream for yourself. I will provide you with helpful ways to build a foundation. Unfortunately, I can't speak with you to see how far along you have come. Only you can hold yourself accountable and for good reason. You are the only one who will become wealthy as a result.

Join Us on our Personal Finance Blog: tinbucketfinance.com

Part I

Chapter 1

Where your money goes each month.

Do you have a pad of paper and a pen or pencil? Good. Let's get started.

The first of the 4 key areas is the most important. What you will learn in this section will create the strength and stability of your future financial home. There are three other key areas but the first one will set the tone and tempo for all the remaining wisdom you will gain from this book.

I hope I am communicating the importance this deserves. You may not immediately understand how this is the most important, but you will when you finish this book. You will understand even more about how this foundation piece affects and determines everything else you learn about money. The information you learn here, in this chapter, will also underscore the success you have with every other strategy and every other book in this series.

Yes. It is that important.

There is an often-quoted definition of insanity. The definition goes something like this: The definition of insanity is doing the same thing over and over again and expecting a different result. I bring this up not to say that you are insane. I bring it up to highlight the notion of change. Reading this book will require you to change some things about yourself, about how you live your life, and about money. These changes require doing some things in a different way because you are looking for a different result. I promise that the changes asked of you will not be big or difficult to achieve. Often, making a small change, when it is the correct change, can have enormous and positive results. This is what I will be asking of you: to make small changes.

The changes I will ask of you may take some effort to accomplish, however, at least in the beginning. After all, if you didn't need help with your finances, if you were already trained and knowledgeable about this, then you wouldn't be reading this book. Keep an open mind, of course, to the changes I am suggesting and then make the decision for yourself.

The First Step.

You may or may not realize it but every profitable company in the world creates a Cash Flow Statement on a regular basis. This is a record of what money was spent and where it was spent, and how much money was taken in and where it came from. They use this information to enable them to make fact-based decisions for the company and with the resources available to them. I understand that you are not a company but you need to make decisions about money that are fact-based. The only way to do that is to create a Cash Flow Statement for yourself and it is relatively easy. Once you do create one, you will be able to make decisions about your money that are rational. You will be taking full responsibility about where your money goes and, hopefully, where it will not go in the future.

A Cash Flow Statement is a complex word for a simple idea. It is simply the calculation of what was spent and what was earned. This will be the simplest definition that will guide you while you create one for yourself.

One of the things I know about people is that they already have an intuitive understanding of earning and spending when it is *their* money. Most people – certainly, nearly every adult in the world – understands that money is a medium of exchange. We exchange money – dollars, pounds, yen, etc. – for goods and services that we require or desire. Most people have a general idea of what they spend on certain things. The Cash Flow Statement will reveal exactly what is spent on everything. No guesswork. No pipedreams. Just facts.

Most of what we do every day involves an exchange. Most importantly, the biggest exchange in our lives is the accepted agreement we have with our employers. Both you and the employer have agreed to exchange their money for your time. You accepted the exchange when you said yes to the job. The same is true for everything you spend money on. The price of flour, or milk, or bread determines the accepted rate of exchange. You give the cashier money and they let you walk out of the store with groceries. Simple, right?

What most people do not consciously realize is that every exchange involves a decision on our part that is based on fact or belief. We decide if the exchange is worth making based on how we want our money to be used. We decide if the price of milk is acceptable. We decide how much our wages should be. Unfortunately, we often believe our wages should be more than the employer believes. Often, too, we accept the price of milk without realizing there may be less expensive options that are easily found. A cash flow statement will allow you to see how you have been making these decisions, and how you will make these decisions in the future.

In the first and most important section of this book, I am going to show you how you will be able to make better decisions with your money. I am going to turn you into a fact-based decision maker.

In any exchange there is someone who profits and, sometimes, someone who doesn't. Often both parties profit but only when both are making fact-based decisions. When the decision is not based on fact, but on impressions or feelings or beliefs, or *convenience*, the outcome is often not profitable for one or both of the parties involved. If this happens to you, I am going to help you change that.

The best decision makers are fact-based decision makers. They understand and know the facts and make rational decisions based on those facts. Those who do not are usually making decisions irrationally and unprofitably.

I present you with a choice to test your understanding so far.

Do you wish to make rational decisions about your money – that is, fact-based decisions - and profit from the exchanges you encounter, or would you like to make these decisions irrationally and simply take your chances and not understand if you profited or lost money on the exchange? If you are still reading, I already know the answer.

How to be a Great Decision Maker.

I wrote earlier about why companies create a Cash Flow Statement so they can make fact-based decisions. These decisions create the exchanges that this company makes. Their success or failure as a business is determined by the quality of those decisions.

The facts they rely upon are the results of the most recent Cash Flow Statement. They tally up all the things their company spent money on, and equally tally up all the money they brought in and compare the two. You already do this to some degree. The difference is that you may be making decisions based not on the purchases you have made in the past but simply based on what is left in your checking account at the end of the month.

If you knew how much you could afford to spend on groceries every month, and you knew how much you had already spent on everything else, making a purchasing decision at the grocery store would be simple, right?

Creating a Cash Flow Statement for ourselves is much easier than it is for that fictional company I keep talking about. If you are ready to create your own Cash Flow Statement for yourself then keep reading. If not, take a break, think about what you've read so far, and decide if you want to start making decisions about your money based on fact or belief.

Chapter 2

Creating a Cash Flow Statement

Welcome back. Relax. This is going to be easy.

The first thing I need you to do is collect the last three months of checking account statements from your bank, preferably printed on paper. Specifically, you must collect statements from the accounts that record where you spend your money. If there are multiple banks, then three months of statements from each. If there are other ways you spend money, such as using PayPal when you are online, please collect the previous three months of statements from them too.

You must have a record of what and where you spent your money.

The second thing to do is to collect the last three months of paystubs from your job. You are either paid every two weeks, twice a month, or, in rare situations, once a month. In either case, collect as many of these as you can but no more than for three consecutive months.

For your checking account statements and your paystubs, it is best if they are complementary; that is, they display information for the same time period.

Congratulations! These are the only documents that you will need to create a Cash Flow Statement.

The next step is to look at each bank statement and categorize each item on the statement. For example, your debit card purchase at the supermarket for $57.36 (an example only) should be labeled "Food" or "Groceries." Make a note of the category for every item on the bank statement and do this on each of the bank statements that you collected. I have created an abbreviated list below to give you some ideas about categories. Your list may include category names that are not on this list. However, every item that records something must be recorded in one of the categories.

Category List:

- Groceries
- Car Fuel
- Utilities (gas and electric, water, garbage)
- Clothes
- Travel
- Rent/Mortgage
- Credit Card Payments
- Car Payments
- Other Loans
- Etc.

Note: For ATM transactions such as withdrawals, simply use the category "cash". We will deal with this mystery soon.

Also note: For items on your bank statements that indicate a deposit, simply categorize this item as "Deposit". These items will be used later.

Make sure you have that pad of paper and a pen or pencil. You may also need to pick up a calculator at this point. You probably have one as an app on your smart phone.

You will want to add up all the items under each of the category names and divide by 3. This is your monthly average spending for this category. For now, stay with a small list of categories. It will be simpler this way but you must include every purchase you have made. Later, after you have created a Cash Flow Statement by hand and are ready to move on to software that will do it for you, you can expand the categories and become much more precise using that tool.

List the categories on a sheet of paper and calculate the average amounts of spending for each (total for 3 months divided by 3 months). Then, go to your paystubs and record as spending those things that are withheld from your Gross Earnings. List them as a category labeled "payroll". This will include all the items that are withheld on your paystub. For example, state and local taxes, federal income taxes, FICA, etc. If you contribute to a 401(K) plan you should see this contribution listed on the paystub and as an expense on your new Cash Flow Statement. List these items on the pad of paper with all the other categories of things you spend money on.

On a separate piece of paper, or underneath the list of categories of spending, write down the average gross income over three months. This is your average income before any deductions like taxes, 401(k) contributions, health insurance, etc. For many people, especially those on salary at work, their income does not vary from one month to the next. For others who are paid an hourly wage, the gross amount of income will fluctuate. You need to know what the average will be in any case.

Have you totaled everything? What is the result? Does your income exceed your expenses? The answer to this is the first piece of information that we need to build wealth. If you have money left over at the end of the month then Congratulations! You are a part of a small fraction of people in this country that live within their means.

Now, for the readers who see the problem immediately because they, on average, are spending more than they make each month, relax. By reading this book, and specifically this section, you are going to learn how easy it is to live within your means – ie. Spend less than you make.

You have created a Cash Flow Statement for yourself. You can see what you spend money on and how much you bring in from employment. Money in. Money out.

<u>Special Note:</u> Do you remember the thought experiment earlier? Do you remember the feeling of being able to keep all of your income? After creating a Cash Flow Statement, you can see that you are able to keep only a small fraction of your income as it stands right now. We are going to focus on that and create more money for you at the

end of every month. We are going to move closer and closer to that thought-experiment's dream.

Chapter 3

A Short Story of Two Brothers

Let's take a break for a moment. I have a short story to tell you. So sit back and relax.

I grew up in a family with two brothers. My older brother is five years older than I. My younger brother is two years younger. I was in the middle, and if you share this particular burden, we both know what it is like.

Many years ago, my younger brother and I went to New York City during the summer break from school. We lived with my older brother who was just beginning his acting career. He is still an actor and I see him on television and in movies all the time. But that is a story for another time.

My younger brother and I had jobs in New York that summer. He worked for a political group and I went to work at a financial brokerage firm.

Every two weeks, both of us would be paid and both of us cashed our paychecks before we paid any bills. When each of us would return home with our paychecks turned into cash, we would immediately begin to divide up the cash into separate envelopes for every expense we needed to pay. My younger brother, Charlie, had a couple of expenses I did not, and vice versa.

At the end of the month, both Charlie and I had a handful of envelopes with specific amounts of cash in each. One envelope was for rent. Another envelope was for groceries. And still another envelope was for other specific expenses. When we needed to pay a bill, like the rent, we would use what we had set aside in that specific envelope. In this way, he and I could determine where our money went and how it was spent. We also knew from one moment to the next what we could spend on other things like going to the movies, or finding a new cafe, or whatever our hearts desired during our summer in the Big Apple.

We knew from one moment to the next if spending money on fun things, ie. our "wants", was advisable or even possible. We had to pay the rent first. And we had to have money for food. My older brother depended on his two younger brothers to pay their way.

At the end of the summer, when all three of us were about to part company and return to our lives, we were very pleased. Over the summer, and because we had paid such close attention to where our money went and how it was spent, there was a significant stack of cash remaining for both myself and my younger brother. My older brother was not especially pleased unfortunately. He had to pay all of the rent after we left.

Going back to school became easy. Charlie and I both knew where we would get the money to buy books, meet up with friends, and pay for much of the unexpected things that come up during the first few weeks of college. Tuition was paid as well with some help from our parents.

During that summer, we had paid attention to our future.

I am telling you this story to dramatize the importance of paying attention. Neither of us were accountable to anyone else. No one was looking over our shoulders to make sure we paid our bills (except my older brother who appreciated the help paying rent). No one reminded us to divide up our paychecks into envelopes or to pay for the "needs" before anything else.

We had a budget. We had income. The remaining money was the wealth we had created that summer. That wealth made going to college easy and affordable. My younger brother eventually became a high school teacher - an occupation that he is especially suited for. I became a financial advisor and writer. He tells me I am suited to that kind of work as I remind him how proud I am of him.

I am telling you this story for 2 reasons. The first is to characterize how "paying attention to your money" can create a relative amount of wealth in a very short period of time; and, second, to demonstrate how easy it really is.

You are responsible for what happens to your hard-earned money. You are also responsible from this moment forward for what you learn and how you apply that learning in your life.

Chapter 4

Creating a Budget

The next step is to create a budget. This is a tool that will help you do the most with the money you have every month. Please remember: the word *budget* brings to mind a sense of drudgery and restrictions to most people, even to you I would suspect. This exercise is about your money and, therefore, your life. Since it is your money and these are the choices and decisions that you make, you have every right to ignore your budget once it is created. The consequences are, therefore, obvious.

The difference between a budget and a cash flow statement is simple to understand. The cash flow statement is about the past – what has happened before you started reading this book. The budget is about the future – what will happen while you read this book and thereafter.

Creating a Budget is simple. The Second Step.

On the Cash Flow Statement, you have a list of categories. Next to each category name you have listed an average monthly amount. The budget will look similar as we are going to use these same categories to determine, not only what you spend, but what you can afford to spend in each area. So, on a separate sheet of paper, list all the categories from top to bottom that appear on the Cash Flow Statement.

Here's the trick: for each item on your new budget, take the amount in each category from the Cash Flow Statement, subtract $25 from the average amount spent over 3 months, and then round up the number to the nearest multiple of $25. This should be only slightly less than your average spending over the last three months.

An example: On your cash flow statement, you list the category <u>Car Fuel</u> and have an average amount of $167 spent over each of the previous three months. Subtract $25. This now equals $142. Round up this number to come to $150. This is your budgeted amount you can spend each month on Car Fuel.

Do this same calculation for each category. For those categories that don't change from one month to the next, list them anyway. The budgeted amount will be the same that you are required to spend, such as Rent. Now, total up all of these categories. If the amount of budgeted expenses is more than you bring in from work, go through this process again paying specific attention to categories where you have control about how much is spent. You will need to lower the amount budgeted for that item. For example, gourmet coffee from the local barista, or clothes, or groceries are good places to look. You must bring the total of these budgeted expenses down to an amount that is less than you make from your job.

Do you remember when I mentioned the category of "cash"? This is the money you spend without a record such, as ATM withdrawals, of where it was spent. My recommendation is for you to go "cash-less" for the next few months. Using a debit card will create a more precise record and reveal where this "cash" is really being spent.

If you can't do this, then you will need to create your own records. The best way is to get a receipt for everything you buy with cash. Or, keep a piece of paper in your pocket with a pen. When you make a purchase and use cash, write down how much, where, and when.

*****

While writing this section, I imagine there are several types of readers. There are some who naturally spend less than they make. There are others, the vast majority, who spend exactly what they make each month. And then, there are some who are making less than they spend each month.

For the first two groups, all of the information in this book still applies to you. Just because you are spending less than you make does not mean that there aren't expenses you could make smaller and increase the amount you have left over each month. For those readers who are in the vast majority who spend exactly what they make each month, the same thing applies. You will need to create "excess income" each month if your goal is to build any amount of personal wealth.

For the last of the three groups: if you are spending more than you make each month, you are probably using credit cards or some other form of debt to make up the difference. And those credit card balances are starting to become large. Don't Panic!!! Beginning in Chapter 6 of this book, we will learn an extremely easy way to eliminate debt of all kinds. For the moment, however, please create a Cash Flow Statement and a Budget. You will thank me later.

This is how a budget really works.

Much like my younger brother and I did during our summer in New York, you need to divide up your paycheck into envelopes. Only now, it will be virtual envelopes and only require you to make notes.

Do you remember earlier in this book I discussed the idea of change? I briefly described how I was going to ask you to make some changes and that it would be simple. In fact, I described the changes as small and I am going to stick to that promise right now.

This is the change I want you to make. I want you to pay attention to how much you spend each pay period. Not each month but every two weeks or so for most people.

The day you get paid is the best day to track what you have been spending against the budget you have created. This will not take much time so pick a time during that day when you have an hour of uninterrupted time.

Most banks in the United States have kept pace with technology and the convenience of online banking is commonplace. You can view your current bank statement in real time, 24 hours a day. If yours does not, I am afraid that you will want to change banks. For the rest of us, on your special "budget" day (or Pay Day), open your current bank statement and go through the same exercise for creating a Cash Flow Statement.

Think of it this way. You are simply trying to stay within your budget based on fact, not feeling.

If you get paid every 2 weeks, or twice a month, you will know right away how close you are to your budget. For example, if you've budgeted $500 per month for groceries and you've already spent $300, you will need to slow down over the next couple of weeks so you don't spend more than the budgeted amount of $500.

I understand that most people, myself included, do not spend money in each category every week. That's ok. The important thing is that by doing this every couple of weeks, on your special "budget" day, you will begin to carry with you a sense of how close you've come to the budget's limit at any given moment. You will begin to make decisions about spending based on facts, no matter whether you have a copy of your Budget in front of you or not.

In essence, you are doing what my younger brother and I did when we worked in New York City during the summer. You are putting cash into virtual envelopes to make sure you pay each of your bills and will have enough to do just that.

So, you have a Budget and are following it, now what?

After a few weeks of working within a Budget, you will begin to discover some things about yourself and money. You will discover how you have been making money decisions all of your life and how you can make decisions in the future. Some of your budget categories are for expenses that you have no control over, such as rent or mortgage, or even a car payment. These expenses are fixed. Nearly all of the other expenses are variable. They change from one month to the next, or from one week to the next. These expenses are the ones you need to concentrate on and make some adult decisions about.

Here is a simpler way to look at your budget.

For each category, I want you to make a small note. I want you to label each category as a "need" or a "want." Those things that you need, such as food, rent, car fuel, will remain as they are for the moment. Everything that you have a choice about, whether to purchase or not, is a "want." These are the items that you will be looking at and deciding how much you really "want" them.

If you really "want" them, then continue spending your hard-earned money to purchase them.

If you realize that you "want" something more, such as a stronger foundation financially, you may choose to stop purchasing these things and postpone the gratification until later.

Do you really need expensive coffee every morning?

Chapter 5

How to Reduce Your Expenses

How much do you spend on groceries? How many options do you have about where you buy these groceries? I happen to live in the country in the State of Montana. We do not have many options as to where we buy food but we do have a few.

There is a large corporate grocery chain in town. When I walk inside there are, it seems, an infinite number of aisles with food of all kinds. They have arranged their shelves to be pleasing to the eye. For myself, I find this to be overwhelming because the assault of color and marketing messages are overpowering. Perhaps that is the intention – overpower the consumer so that they cannot make rational, fact-based decisions about their purchases. Food for thought, so to speak.

There is a choice where I live. There is an employee-owned chain of supermarkets in Montana and one of their stores is a few blocks away from the corporate supermarket. It is a very different experience to shop there. It is also less expensive which is why I go there intentionally.

The downside to this supermarket is the lack of visual impact. There are shelves of food just like in the corporate store but there is very little bright color or dramatic marketing messages present. In fact, one might call it drab compared to the corporate store. I spend significantly less here than at the supermarket that wishes to overwhelm me when I walk in.

I am telling this small story to make a point. Big corporate supermarkets are run by very intelligent people. That's how they got to be big. There is a reason why the colors are bright and the floors are sparking clean. There is a reason why the produce is arranged in an attractive way. The entire impression received by a shopper is designed to overwhelm them so that they do not make rational decisions about their purchases. Keep this in mind when you go shopping. No matter what retail store you are in, the way it is arranged, the colors you see, the attitude of the salespeople, is entirely designed to remove rational decision making from your experience. It is designed to encourage you to spend more than you would have done otherwise.

Where you spend your money is a choice. You make this choice every time you shop. If you can change how you make these decisions, choosing to purchase the same things but at a lower cost, you will see a dramatic increase in the amount of money left over every month. It will be easier to stay within your budget and you will be able to begin building wealth for yourself and your family (or your future family).

Look closely at every item in your budget, even the ones that you believe you must pay, such as rent. Could you find a cheaper place to live? How about Clothes? Can you do without buying new clothes for a month or so? Are you a coffee drinker like me? I really enjoy going to one of the big chain coffee shops because of the quality of the coffee. I also learned that I can get the same coffee in the supermarket and brew it at home and save an unbelievable amount of money each month.

Was this a good decision?

If you did not create a Cash Flow Statement or a Budget as you were reading, this would be a great time to do just that. Here's a summary:

- Collect three months of bank statements.
- Collect three months of paystubs.
- Categorize each item on each bank statement.
- For each category, calculate the average of 3 months.
- For each category, subtract $25, then round up.
- This is your budget.

Your Ongoing Homework:

I did say that there would be some work required of you, didn't I?

Again, please do not worry. The ongoing homework is easy. In order for you to build wealth now and in the future, you will rely on your income to create excess money. In other words, you will need to spend less than you make. This is why I have walked you through creating a Cash Flow Statement and a Budget. The Budget is there to help you make decisions about each and every one of your purchases.

If you are living from paycheck to paycheck, spending exactly what you make, or you are spending less or more than you make, you will need to reduce your expenses in order to have extra money each month to begin building wealth.

Here is your homework assignment.

For each category in your budget, I want you to use your creativity to find ways to spend less. For each category, you may find that not spending money on that particular item is the best way to go. Or, you may find a way to spend on that category but in a different way or at a different place. Your creativity will carry you a long way if you allow it to do so. Your homework assignment is to find a way to spend less in every category that you have some control over and even those categories that you don't, like Rent (Can you find a cheaper place to live?).

You have more control than you may believe.

In the next section, I will be helping you with the biggest problem that most people face: *debt*. If you have debts and they showed up on your Cash Flow Statement, especially if the debts are with credit card companies, I will show you a simple and very effective way to eliminate them forever.

For now, complete your Cash Flow Statement and your Budget. Go through the homework assignment over the next week or so. Once done, you are in a much stronger position to begin building wealth.

Disclaimer: Any financial advice, technique, or opportunity revealed in this series of books or anything pertaining to financial markets, in part or as a whole, is purely for informational purposes only. Any insight gained by the reader is similarly for informational purposes and the author of this manuscript does not take responsibility for how this information is used.

Part II

Chapter 6

Debt Elimination

So far, in Part I, we went through the process of determining where your money goes each month. Nothing could be more important to building wealth for you and your family. Your job, or profession, is what will drive your effort to build wealth. With the strategies in this first book on wealth building, you will learn how to do the most with what you have.

You may be wondering why an entire section of this book is dedicated to Debt Elimination. It is important, you say, but is it worth writing about and taking up more than 25% of the entire manuscript? My answer is simple and direct:

Yes. It is.

And you will see why in a moment.

Debt is money that you have borrowed and are in the process of paying back. There are car loans, credit cards, personal loans, mortgages, and even unpaid taxes that the IRS would feel so much more comfortable if you actually paid back (I make jokes).

There is "good" debt and "bad" debt. It is not hard to figure out which is which.

Examples of "good" debt are loans or obligations that allow you to acquire something that will retain its value, or increase in value, while you are paying off the loan. The most obvious example of "good" debt is borrowing money to purchase a house. Not only is it your home, but it is also a physical asset that will increase in value over time with a high degree of certainty.

We are going to devote an entire section of this book to the elimination of "bad" debt. It is such a plague upon the efforts of people who wish to build wealth, and anyone else for that matter, that it deserves this much attention. After the exercise in Part I where you calculated a Cash Flow Statement and created a Budget, if you found that you are using a significant portion of your paycheck to pay off these financial traps, then this section is what you came here to read.

Here are some statistics to chew on before we begin:

1. # credit cards in the US: In 2018, there were 1.12 billion credit cards in the USA.

2. Average # credit cards per person: In 2020, there were 2.35 credit cards per person in the USA as an average. This average is growing.

3. Average balance per person: In 2020, the average credit card debt balance was $5,551.

One thing that I hoped you noticed when you went through the process of totaling up your expenses and comparing the total to your "take home" pay, is that there are several individual expenses that you can do without such as debt payments. In Part II, we are going to examine this peculiar expense for two reasons. First, it is so prevalent in people's budget; and second, it is so unnecessary.

I can think of only two examples of debt that involves something that will appreciate at some point in the future - i.e. "Good Debt." The first is debt used to purchase a thriving business. The assets and continued business revenues are what you own. If you are successful, the business will grow and the debt will be paid off at some point in the near future. When that happens, you are left with the entire value of the business. This is a great example of how wealth is built.

The other example is debt you take on to purchase a house, especially if the debt is long term, such as a thirty-year mortgage.

Before you nod your head in agreement and believe that your home mortgage is such a great deal, there is something you need to understand. In both instances of "good" debt described above there is also risk. There is a risk that if you purchase a thriving business that it will not continue to thrive once you take ownership. There could be an economic downturn that causes your new business to fail through no fault of your own. There could be hidden problems in the business that were unexpected and hazardous. If this happens, the "good" debt can become "bad" debt very quickly.

Likewise, there is risk when you purchase a house. There are dozens of ways that a house can lose value either in the short term or long term. So, in both cases, debt is still something to be very careful with and understand that risk exists in either case.

I remember years ago, long before the mortgage and housing crisis began in late 2008, I tried to describe the inherent risk in homeownership to a real estate broker. He laughed. When he was finished chuckling, and with a modest amount of mockery, he said "No one has ever lost money in their homes." And then the housing crisis appeared.

So much for certainty and the denial of risk in any venture that involves the exchange of money.

From 2008 until sometime in 2011, millions of people lost their homes due to foreclosure when many people discovered the downside to a variable interest rate mortgage. In the beginning of the mortgage cycle, the interest rate was low and affordable. When the lending institutions and banks began having trouble with subprime mortgages and foreclosures, they tried to make up for their losses by increasing the interest rates on variable rate mortgages to the fullest extent of the law. Before many people could respond, their mortgage payments were far above what they could afford and soon they were forced to suffer a foreclosure and lost their homes. All the equity that they were enjoying only a year or two before, went up in smoke. They lost everything. The down-payment that they spent months or years accumulating and the mortgage that they had been paying on for the last few years were both gone.

Risk exists everywhere. Never forget this.

It is ironic that I have been writing about "good" debt and done nothing but paint a gloomy picture. I do so only to inform. If you own your home and are paying a mortgage payment every month, you shouldn't worry as long as it stays affordable.

The flip side of the housing and mortgage crisis is that for those who could hold onto their homes, they are still living in them and still paying off the mortgage. In most cases, they have seen an appreciation in value although less than they were expecting. This is only true because they were able to hold on until the crisis was over.

Chapter 7

Let's talk about "bad" debt.

Credit cards are what most economists describe as "consumer" debt. Within this description, there may also be personal loans, car loans, and any type of debt that involves a depreciation of value in the object purchased. The car loan is a perfect example of this. No one has ever seen the value of their car appreciate after they purchased it. Even the so-called "classic" cars are still not worth what they were when they were new. Don't believe me? Do the calculation for yourself. And don't forget to factor in the effects of inflation on the original price of that "classic" car you have dreamed about. Trust me, it is not worth what it once was no matter what someone is willing to pay for it.

You need a car, however. The car, itself, is what gets you to work so you can make a living, pay for groceries, the mortgage, and anything else you or your family needs. You "needed" a car so you accepted a car loan. The good news is that the depreciation of the car is equal to the utility that you use every day. It is a fair deal when you understand that a car, just like a suit of clothes, or a stack of ribeye steaks, is a consumable object. Unfortunately, borrowing money to purchase something that will be used up is often a financial hole that is difficult to escape.

The worst form of debt is innocently sitting in your wallet or purse.

It's a pretty little thing, isn't it? Shiny and colorful. It may even have a wonderfully inspiring picture embedded in the plastic that you look at every time you pull it out to purchase something new (sarcasm is intended here).

Make no mistake. Credit cards are what are holding you back, no matter how much wealth you have created or how much you earn annually.

Even though you accepted the credit card because you wanted to be able to purchase things or experiences before you had the money to do so. Yes. You purchased something even though you didn't have the money to do so. Admit it.

The consequences of this choice have brought you to where you are right now.

Not sure where that is exactly? How much do you pay the credit card companies each month to eventually pay off this debt even though the card is "maxed out" and you can't use it to buy anything? And what do you get in return for this payment each month? Nothing. This is where you are. This is the consequence of credit card debt.

Don't worry. There is a solution.

I am going to show you an easy way to eliminate this debt and, once done, encourage you to never get caught in this trap again.

A number of years ago, there was a law to prevent usury. This is not a word that most people are familiar with. Usury is the abuse of lenders upon the borrowers and the law prevented lenders from charging too much interest. The maximum interest rate allowed by law was once 21%. That was the highest interest rate they, or anyone else, could charge to loan money. The law prevented usury abuse.

The law was rescinded in 1999. Nowadays, lenders can charge whatever they wish. Once the law was removed, can you guess what happened to consumer loan interest rates? Up or down? Silly question (Yes. More sarcasm).

So, why would anyone accept a credit card that charged them 30% annually on the balance? Another good question. Plenty of people do accept this agreement. This is where they get into trouble and it's not their fault, really, as I will explain in a moment.

Let's use a reasonably realistic example. Let's say you have a credit card with a maximum limit of $5,000. You believe yourself to be a responsible adult and don't let the card's balance go beyond $3,000. Once there, you stop using it. You might even take it out of your wallet or purse and drop the card in a desk drawer. Out of sight, out of mind, right?

Furthermore, let's say that the credit card company is charging you an interest rate of 24% APR (annual percentage rate). Here's what this really means, and how it influences your future, even without the addition of annual fees and occasional maintenance fees:

Your minimum payment each month: $120

The amount of this payment that goes toward paying off the balance: $4.80

The percentage of this payment that goes toward paying the interest: 96.00%

# of months to pay off the entire balance: 137 (Eleven years, 5 months)

Note: The percentage of the minimum payment that goes toward the balance is determined by the credit card issuer. This percentage fluctuates from issuer to issuer. 4% is used here as an average amount found by comparing over 10 different credit card issuers. Over time, the minimum payment will decrease as the balance owed decreases.

If all you can do is pay the minimum each month, you are throwing your money away. Simple as that. You will end up paying thousands of dollars on top of the credit card's balance when you finally pay off the entire card. Often, the total amount that you pay over the course of paying off the debt will equal the amount of the balance. You borrowed $3,000 and will eventually pay $6,000 (approximately).

Was it worth it to be able to spend when you didn't have the cash?

Now that you know and understand the danger, perhaps I can write about why we have these disastrous financial instruments in the first place. Without going into the history, or the Diner's Club Card as the first such malicious arrangement, I believe you already know the answer to whether you are ready to admit it or not.

You were sold on the marketing promise these companies made to you. They promised, either overtly or by implying such things through imagery and glamorous soundtracks, a life of *affluence.*

It didn't matter to them or to you whether you could afford an afluent life but the offer was made and you accepted. You told yourself you could handle it. You may have told yourself that you needed the card, that it would help build your credit rating, or it would help if you overspent in any given month. It would smooth things out and make you more financially stable. Do any of these rationalizations sound familiar?

Here's the good news. Well, several pieces of good news, actually.

The first spot of good news is that this is entirely fixable. You can eliminate the debt once and for all and you can start enjoying extra money each month to build wealth and have the life you really want and do so in a realistic way. I will present to you a simple plan that has worked for actual people I advised while I was a financial advisor. This plan works and I'll show you how.

There is relief. Hang on.

The second spot of good news is that the debt you are currently paying off is not your fault. The marketing efforts and messages of credit card companies are designed to tap into our base instincts. We are wired by our species' history on this planet to want more - more food, more security, more ability to breed - in order to survive. The myth of affluence is based on these simple human, and utterly inescapable, instinctual drives. And the credit card companies know this. The level of debt that you are suffering from is not your fault.

The only fault that can be given to you is your refusal to want a way out.

Well? What do you want to do?

Do you remember the short example I used above? You know, the credit card balance is $3,000 and the minimum payments made each month do very little to pay down the balance? We are going to use this example again.

Here's what this level of debt actually does to you by comparing two scenarios.

Instead of being required to pay off a credit card, you don't have the debt and are able to invest $120 per month into a retirement program such as a Roth IRA.

$120 per month invested into a Roth IRA (for this example only) creates a contribution of $1440 per year.

At $1440 per year, after 10 years, and with normal appreciation of 8%, the entire investment equals $ 21,851.39, with the total amount contributed over ten years of $ 14,400.

Now, let's compare apples to apples, as they say. Let's compare the credit card described earlier that takes 137 months to pay off.

Since the credit card companies require a minimum payment each month that is based on a small percentage of the remaining balance plus interest, the minimum payment will go down as the balance-owed goes down.

How long does it take to pay off the credit card if you pay $120 per month, instead of the shrinking "minimum payment"? This will provide a better "apples to apples" comparison.

It will take you approximately 3 years to pay off this debt. Actually, on the 35th month you will pay off the debt completely with a last payment of $0.33. So, actually you could pay off this debt in 34 months. (Did I mention that I am an amateur numbers geek?)

After 34 months of contributing to the Roth IRA with $120 per month, how much have you accumulated? At the end of the 34th month, at an average growth rate of 8% annually, your Roth IRA has grown to $ 4,699.08. You contributed a total of $ 4,080.00

The choice is yours.

You can be the person who continues to pay down a credit card after purchasing something that they could not afford (very much like the people with 1.12 billion credit cards) and continue paying them $120 per month when, after 34 months, you have paid off the debt but you have nothing to show for it.

Or, you can be the person who contributes $120 per month into a Roth IRA for 34 months and end up accumulating $ 4,699.08.

After 34 months (nearly 3 years), which person do you want to be? Remember, the key to building wealth over your lifetime is to learn how to make fact-based decisions about your money.

Before I go into the plan and strategy of paying off all of your credit card and personal loans, I want to open up your thinking about the thing that got you in trouble in the first place: the desire for an abundant life. I realize I have changed the word in this case but many people use these two words interchangeably and this is a mistake.

Affluence is about wealth. Abundance is about being realistically satisfied with what you have.

Most of us will never reach the levels of an Affluent life. Most of us will never be in the top 1% of wealth owners in this country. But we can have an abundant life where the wealth we do have provides us everything we need or could want. Your dreams are not unrealistic. The message you are hearing from the media, from marketing agencies, and social media are wildly unrealistic, however, and unfortunately this message colors how we understand the concept of abundance.

Warning: if you are setting your sights on an Affluent Life, you should stop reading right now. You are either on your way already, or, you are simply not recognizing the realities of life. I do not deal in pipe dreams or fantastical wishes. I deal with what is possible which, surprisingly, encompasses an entire universe of possibilities.

Now that I have gotten that out of the way . . . there's one more thing.

If you have spent any time online and researched how to get your finances in order then undoubtedly you have come across some of the more popular blogs and websites that claim to be focused on Personal Finance. Some of these resources are excellent. Some, however, have an ulterior motive.

You may have noticed that on some of these websites, there is always a section on Credit Cards. The creators of the websites include this category in their blog posts for one simple reason. They are trying to put a positive spin on the credit card and the popular tendency of people to spend more than they make.

Sounds irrational, doesn't it? Well, there is a rational explanation. For them, at least. These websites are paid extremely well by the credit card companies. If a viewer on their website is reading one of their blog posts and clicks on a link to find more information about a credit card, and then provides them with some personal information, the website is paid a finder's fee (or affiliate commission).

Is it any surprise that a website claiming to be focused on your financial success is also paid by the same companies that want nothing more than to take a piece of your income every single month and diminish your ability to accumulate wealth? It is not a surprise no matter how shocking the revelation of this relationship really happens to be.

My intention is not to scare you. My intention is to simply open your eyes.

I want to congratulate you for reading this far. I have painted a gloomy picture in many examples in this book, and probably put you to sleep with the numbers in these examples. You should be congratulated for staying with it. I promise that there will not be any more gloomy scenarios. Along with this congratulations, I now offer a reward.

Chapter 8

The Solution and The Remedy

Eliminating debt, specifically consumer debt, is a relatively easy thing to do even if you have been struggling until now. You must complete a Cash Flow Statement and establish a Budget, however. The remainder of this section will not work for you if you have not done this.

To eliminate credit card or consumer debt, there are three ways to go about it. The first two are what amateurs recommend. The third is what professionals recommend.

Guess which one I want you to follow?

The First Method: there is a popular idea out there, mostly promoted by people on the internet with little or no experience, that involves consolidating all of your debt into one single account, or one single debt. The attractive idea, I believe, is that if there is only one payment to make, one debt effectively, then it will be easier to deal with. In some way, the entire debt will be easier to manage.

Nothing could be farther from the truth.

When you consolidate your credit cards into one single card you have done nothing to reduce the balance owed nor the amount you will pay each month. In fact, there will be fees to do this consolidation and you will, therefore, increase the balance. Perhaps this is why most credit card companies continue to recommend this strategy.

If you find a way to consolidate all these cards into a single card that has a lower interest rate then you have done nothing you couldn't do before consolidation. If you qualify for a lower rate, negotiate with the current credit card companies to lower the rate on the current card or cards. In most instances, they will comply in order to retain you as a customer.

Consolidation does nothing but make it appear to be easier. Ironically, the desire is to make it easier to pay off, yet it is hard work and time consuming to consolidate all of your credit cards into one single card. This is a fool's errand and is promoted heavily by the credit card companies themselves.

The Second Method: This is an equally amateurish attempt. Listing your credit cards in order of highest to lowest interest rates and then trying to pay them off in that order accomplishes very little. The idea behind this strategy is to eliminate the biggest interest rate burden in the bunch first and then move on to the next one. This is the opposite of consolidation. Dividing to conquer may save a few dollars but, for most people, the higher rate cards have the highest balances and the effort to pay it off first makes the whole process take longer and most people lose focus and eventually fail.

Note: There is another strategy I have found that closely resembles the professional strategy you are about to read about. This strategy is proposed by a very successful personal finance blogger and podcaster named Dave Ramsey. He calls it the Snow Ball Strategy. At its most basic level, this strategy involves listing your debts from top to bottom, in order of smallest to largest debts. Then, focusing all of your extra income on the first debt, paying it off, and then moving on to the second item.

This strategy falls short in one crucial area as you will find out here.

Here is what professionals recommend:

Step 1.

In the same manner as creating a Cash Flow Statement, I want you to collect the most recent credit card statement (or statement from a personal loan) for each of the credit cards you have. On a sheet of paper, I want you to list each credit card by name (column #1), current balance owed (column #2), and minimum monthly payment (column #3). Go ahead and add other debts to this list including personal loans, bank loans, mortgages, car loans, etc. This strategy works no matter what kind of debt you have.

Step 2.

In a fourth column, I want you to calculate the "Balance owed to Minimum Payment" ratio. For example, if the balance owed is $1,000 and the minimum payment is $25, then the ratio is 40:1. Do this calculation for each of the credit cards and consumer loans.

Step 3.

You will need to recreate the list one more time. For this second draft, list each debt from the lowest to highest ratios calculated in Step 2. For example, if there are three credit cards and the ratios are 12:1, 15:1, and 17:1, then they are in the right order.

Note: Here is where the Professional's strategy differs from Dave Ramsey's. When you are trying to pay off debt with a small amount of extra cash each month, it is crucial to have your money work as hard as possible. Each buck has to have the biggest bang possible.

By utilizing the ratios of Balance owed to Minimum Payments, you are giving these dollars the biggest bang for each buck. As the amount available increases over time, your power to pay off the debt is maximized. Just paying off the smallest debt first, and therefore the largest paid off last, does not necessarily maximize the effort you are putting into this.

There is one more part of the strategy. In your Cash Flow Statement and your Budget, it will be necessary to create some excess income, or money left over at the end of the month. It can be $20 or $100 but by creating a budget, and sticking to it, you will determine what that number can be. This number is the amount you will dedicate toward paying off the credit cards in addition to the minimum monthly payments you are already paying.

Step 4.

You have your list of debt and the order in which you plan to pay each one off. For each month in this exercise, you will make the minimum monthly payments for each one except the first one on the list.

For this card, the first one you will pay off, I want you to add the amount you have discovered is extra income each month. As I said before, it could be $20 or $100 or something specific to you and your life. Your Budget and Cash Flow Statement will show what that amount can be realistically.

Each month, pay the first card on the list in an amount equal to the minimum monthly payment plus the extra amount available. Make a note on the list of debts how much that combined amount is. For example, the minimum monthly payment is $52 and the extra income available is $38. The total payment to this credit card each month is now $90. You will pay $90 every month to this debt until it is eliminated even if the minimum monthly payment decreases.

It may take a month, or it may take several months, to pay off this card. Keep at it. Don't lose hope. The effect of this strategy takes some time to be felt and seen. Once you have paid off this first card, recalculate the list of remaining debt in the four columns as before from lowest to highest ratios. Your minimum payments may have changed already.

Step 5.

You have paid off the first credit card. Now, add the $90 from the example above to the minimum monthly payment of the second card. The minimum payment is, in this example, $43. The total payment you will make is therefore $43 plus $90, or $133. Make a note on the list of this last number. Once you pay off the second card, recalculate the list in four columns from lowest to highest ratios and repeat this process.

I think you can see how, from one month to the next, the amount you are using to pay off the top card is growing. This momentum is what will accelerate the process.

For example, the third card has a minimum monthly payment of $112. The total amount paid to this credit card debt each month will be $245. Each time you have begun to pay off a new card, you have not had less money each month to spend on the necessities according to your budget. Instead, the payments you have been making have been compounding. This process builds over time. Each time a credit card is paid off, there is more to use to pay off the next one. It creates its own momentum.

This strategy relies heavily on an accurate Cash Flow Statement and realistic Budget. As you can see, the growing amount being used to pay off the credit cards does not impact your budget or reduce the amount available for other purchases. You are beginning to use your money effectively.

However, if you can work creatively to create more excess income each month then the process of eliminating these debts can speed up. For example, reducing your food budget by $100 will create an extra $100 to use for debt elimination, and therefore allow you to reach that point where paying off debts comes sooner.

Depending on how many credit cards you have, this process can take weeks, or months, or years. In order to start building wealth, you must eliminate the "bad" debt that destroys wealth.

Chapter 9

A Short Story of a Former Client

In order to encourage you, I want to relate an experience I had with a client during the time I was a financial advisor. If you find the details of these people's lives to be extreme or unbelievable, I must disappoint you. The only facts in this case study that have been changed are the names of the clients. Everything else is factual and truthful.

I met Lisa and Doug Thompson in late 2007. They were referred to me by another client and I agreed to meet soon after speaking with them over the phone. It was a fall afternoon when we finally sat down in my office. My office had a broad window that looked out over Highway 17 in Silicon Valley, Ca. It was a very nice day.

After some introductions and pleasant talk, I asked them, "How can I help you as a financial advisor?"

Before I could encourage them more, Lisa began to cry. Tears began to fall from her eyes. Doug was a rock and simply sat with a look of frustration on his face, not from his wife but from what I began to learn from Lisa.

"It's, it's, . . . it's the credit cards," she finally blurted out between sobs.

I asked her to explain more in detail. What I learned over the next few minutes affected me greatly as the suffering I imagined in their lives was a tragedy and a testament to their relationship and integrity towards one another.

They explained that there were 27 credit cards and each month 27 credit card statements arrived in the mail. Each month, she said, involved a short period of panic as each of the final days of the month brought half a dozen credit card envelopes. They owed a total of $32,000 to these credit card companies. This was a very bad place to be in, financially and emotionally.

We agreed to meet again in a week when they would bring in copies of their credit card statements and I would look them over to figure out what I could do for them. It wasn't a matter of whether or not they were acceptable to me as clients. I was going to help them and would do everything I could do to find a solution.

Our second meeting was short as the purpose of the meeting was simply to present me with the documents so that I could see exactly what information was available. They were much calmer in this second meeting and I continued to provide encouragement and hope.

Over the next two weeks, I developed the strategy that I have recommended to you in the previous chapters. When Doug and Lisa and I met again, I showed them a realistic plan to pay them off and get out from under this crippling debt. By my calculations, it would take them 18 months. This is, to some people, a long time especially when they would see nearly the same stack of envelopes in the mail each month. Eighteen months is a long time to stick to a single strategy and I was concerned they might not stay with it for that long.

We met again after one month and I was surprised at how they had physically changed for the better. They sat up straight in their chairs. Doug even told a small joke, smiling and looking adoringly at his wife. Lisa was eager to continue, almost obsessively, as she reported to me that they had paid off the first card. Doug admitted that a bottle of champagne had been opened and I encouraged them further to celebrate every time they paid one of them off in the future.

Doug and Lisa, admittedly, did not really want or need a financial advisor. They both had 401(K) plans at work and would resume contributing to them once the credit cards were paid off. They were both in their early 40's so time was on their side to retire comfortably. Neither of them had extravagant tastes and spending was not a problem. They had simply fallen into a trap with the credit cards that many people fall into.

After ten months, I had not met with them for some time. I was curious how their plan, our plan, was turning out so I called them at home. To my surprise, and great satisfaction, Doug told me that they had paid off all of the credit cards except two. And, Doug explained, they would pay those off in the next couple of months.

One Year. 27 credit cards. $32,000 of debt. Miraculous.

I must caution those of you who suffer from this trap and are only now discovering a method to get out of the trap. Doug and Lisa did more than I recommended to pay off this debt. They calculated a cash flow statement, created a budget, and then went further to reduce their expenses. Everything that was left over at the end of the month, after all of their necessary expenses were paid, was committed to paying off the cards and escaping this trap. It took them a year. It might take you a year, or longer, or less time. The method is here for you to copy for yourself. The level of commitment that you bring to this will determine the level of success that you will see.

The silver lining for Doug and Lisa was that since they had been suffering from so much debt, they had become very frugal people out of necessity. Once the debt was removed, they had thousands of dollars each month to direct at retirement savings plans and wealth building investments. They had truly created an abundant life for themselves in only one year.

If you can see, just for a moment, how disastrous credit cards can be to your present and future lives, I hope you can muster the commitment to accomplishing this achievement. All of my hope is with you. All of my encouragement is at your feet. This book is my best effort to reach as many of you as I can and help in whatever way I am able.

I wish you mornings of hope and wonder, afternoons of calm and solace, and evenings of fantastic dreams only you can manifest. Keep reading. There is much more for you in these pages.

Disclaimer: Any financial advice, technique, or opportunity revealed in this series of books or anything pertaining to financial markets, in part or as a whole, is purely for informational purposes only. Any insight gained by the reader is similarly for informational purposes and the author of this manuscript does not take responsibility for how this information is used.

Part III

Chapter 10

Cash Reserves

You will hear this a lot from me in this book: Congratulations!!!!

Why am I congratulating you before you finish this book? Because I know that much of the work I have asked you to do - and it is crucial that you have done it - is dry, and some might say, boring. Hang in there with me. Soon you will start seeing the results and it will no longer be boring or seen as a "chore."

I promise you.

Important: If you are reading this book and not doing the work at each step, that's OK. However, in order to get any benefit from the next two parts, you will need to complete the work in Part I at a minimum. I know. I know. It feels like drudgery, but you are about to see in Part III how beneficial that work will be for you.

Hang in there. Do the work in Part I and Part II and then come back here.

In addition to offering my congratulations, I also offer some pats on the back to those of you (hopefully, everyone) who have done the work in Part I and even in Part II. That stuff was the hardest part, by far.

By completing the work in Part I, you are in the top 10% of adults in this country who have a working budget and use it. Only one person in twenty has a cash flow statement along with a working budget and knows where their money actually goes each month. They, like you, are the ones that are serious about creating wealth for themselves and they, and you, are the ones who will actually do it.

Only one person in 30 has taken effective steps to eliminate their debt. If you have completed the work in Part II, then you can consider yourself to be *extraordinary*. What you have done so far is exceptional and you will see results very soon that make all the work worthwhile.

Let's move forward.

The promise I made to you at the beginning was that the tools and exercises in this book would create a foundation for your efforts to create wealth for you and your family.

There are two parts that remain - one half of the financial foundation - and the importance of putting all four parts into action is beginning to reveal itself.

Cash Reserves.

You have probably heard this term before. If not, you have heard of putting money aside for a rainy day. You may also see this described as Emergency Funds, Rainy Day Money, Cash Reserves, and any number of other descriptions. No matter what it is called, the money that you use to create Cash Reserves will help to protect the wealth you create for the rest of your life.

Cash Reserves do several things.

This money is your safety net in the event that your best asset - your income - diminishes or disappears in any way. This is the money you will use if you lose your job, your employer goes out of business, or there is some event that prevents you from working and earning an income.

Cash Reserves are also used for unexpected expenses such as repair or maintenance on your car, repair or maintenance on your house, or someone in your household develops a health issue that requires money upfront. It may even help if, like me, you have several dogs or cats in the house and one of them becomes ill or injured. Veterinarians cost money and very few of them will allow you to pay over time.

One of the most common needs for emergency funds is when someone needs to buy a plane ticket in order to travel unexpectedly. Most people have a credit card for events like this. We have already discussed the disaster that awaits nearly everyone who accepts a credit card. Cash Reserves can take the place of what the credit card was originally intended to provide in this example.

There are nearly an infinite number of scenarios where an emergency or an unexpected event creates a short-term need for money. Especially for spending that is not in the budget.

Cash Reserves are not really an investment. However, I am going to show you how it can earn adequate amounts of return while at the same time protect you, your family, and your lifestyle.

The most important result of completing the tasks in Part I is to understand the amount of money that you will need. You know how much you need to spend on normal expenses and, by consequence, how much you need to earn as income to maintain the lifestyle you have and the expenses this lifestyle includes.

However . . .

Imagine for a moment that you are laid off from your job.

This is not the worst thing that can happen but let's assume that it takes you three months to find a new job that will pay you the same or more than the job you lost. It may take you more or less time than this to recover but three months is a good benchmark.

How will you pay for your current expenses without an income?

Simple. Create a cash reserve that is equal to three months of your current expenses. Notice that I am not saying "3 months of your income." Before you can spend your income on your expenses, taxes and other withholdings are removed. An adequate amount for many people is three months' worth of *expenses*.

I understand that everyone is different. Some people are single and live alone. They have no one else who is depending on them and the income they earn. Others are married and have children. Perhaps the husband or wife in our imaginary example also works and contributes to paying the expenses but the children don't. They are wholly dependent on the income earned by the parents.

Cash Reserves are extremely important when children are involved.

Normally, I recommend that for a person who is not married and there are no children, they should have three months' worth of their expenses set aside in some form of cash reserves. For the reader who is in a professional occupation, taking three months to find the right job is not unheard of or out of the question.

For those of you who are married and have children, the recommended amount of cash reserves is six months' worth of your expenses. This is doubly important if only one of the parents is working and earning an income. If you lose your job and find a replacement in two or 3 months, that's great. But if it takes longer, or even has the possibility of taking longer, you are protecting your children as well as your lifestyle.

Many people object to this high amount in cash reserves. They claim that their brokerage account or other assets can take the place of reserves and provide the money they need.

Perhaps they can do this but maybe they shouldn't.

An example will illustrate this second protective feature.

Let's say that our imaginary person has expenses of $6,000 per month, nothing in cash reserves, and over $100,000 in an taxable investment account. In this investment account, our imaginary person has invested in stocks, bonds, and mutual funds. This person is not married nor do they have any children.

This person will say that they can always use the assets in their investment account if they get laid off or their employer runs into trouble. They can liquidate the stocks, bonds, or mutual funds into cash if they lose their job for any reason or if an unexpected event or emergency occurs.

This would be a big mistake.

If this person is laid off, it is likely that this is not an isolated incident. It is more likely that it is from an economic downturn.

If the economy is slowing down and their employer needs to cut back, then the stocks and mutual funds they own will be just as likely to go down in value at the same time. I will go into this scenario in much more detail in the second book of our series but, for now, you need to understand that liquidating an investment when it has dropped in value due to economic downturn is the wrong time to do so. In fact, it is the time to begin adding more money to the investment.

Our imaginary person, therefore, is setting themselves up for failure. If they lose their job and liquidate three months' worth of expenses, they may have continued their ability to live the lifestyle they have chosen and pay the expenses of that lifestyle but they have done so at the expense of all of their wealth building efforts.

They would do much better for themselves if they followed strategies that allow them to build an appropriate level of cash reserves over a short period of time and not have to sell their investments at a loss.

Where do you put your cash reserves?

The first place is in a savings account at your bank. How much is entirely up to you but the strategy is to have enough cash on hand to pay your expenses until you can liquidate something else such as a money market fund or a Certificate of Deposit. If you have one month's worth of expenses in your bank savings you can retrieve other funds from other sources long before you need them to cover your bills after the first month.

The second place you can put cash reserves is a Money Market account. Either at your bank or at a brokerage firm, a money market account is very similar to a savings account. There is a guaranteed rate of return, although small, but bigger than from the savings account the bank offers.

You could hold these cash reserves at the brokerage firm where you have your other investment accounts. This would, of course, mean that the cash reserves are set aside from other investments and remain available to you at any time.

Special Circumstances:

1. Creating an adequate level of cash reserves may be difficult if there is only $50 left over every month. Don't panic!!! In the following chapter, I will go into several strategies that will enable you to create the cash reserves you need.

2. If you have reached the point where you have a couple of hundred dollars left over each month, give yourself a pat on the back. You are one of the few people in this world who do not spend more than they make each month, nor do you spend exactly what you make each month. Building cash reserves will be easy for you.

3. If you have begun eliminating your credit card debt and wish to begin creating cash reserves at the same time, you may find that trying to do both is too much to ask. Focus on eliminating the debt first. Once that burden is eliminated, you will probably have plenty left over at the end of the month to build enough cash reserves quickly.

I promised to show you some hidden, or seldom talked about, strategies concerning your checking and savings accounts. Keep in mind, however, that many of the so-called gurus and experts in Personal Finance will try to convince you to stay away from savings accounts because the interest earned is so low and often nearly zero. They believe that your money can and will serve you better somewhere else.

Let's find out the truth, shall we?

Chapter 11

Your Bank: Friend or Foe?

Most banks in this country offer several different types of checking accounts to their new and current customers. In the selection of checking accounts offered, there is, usually, a standard checking account that simply requires $100 or less to open. They have some checks printed for you and issue a debit card as well. Most of us are used to this kind of bank checking account.

There are other accounts they offer. You were offered these alternatives when you became a customer of your bank. You may have ignored them because you couldn't afford to open one of these types of accounts as they required a larger deposit.

The type of checking account that is important to pay attention to is the account that requires a minimum deposit to a savings account and is larger than the standard account requires. This type of account will eliminate all maintenance fees in your checking and/or savings account. At my bank, this account requires a minimum deposit of $1,500 into a savings account that is connected to the checking account to cover any overdrafts there. In exchange for this higher deposit, the standard monthly maintenance fee on the checking and savings accounts are removed. At my bank, this combined fee is $17 per month.

This is the important part.

In exchange for depositing $1,500 into a savings account, I am no longer required to pay $17 per month to maintain the checking and savings accounts. In other words, the $1,500 in savings is earning $17 per month, or $202 per year. This is equal to a 13.46% rate of return on the money in savings, not including the declared interest rate on the account which, in this case, is 0.5%.

So much for the Personal Finance gurus that say savings accounts are a waste of money.

But wait. There is more.

Many people, and I'm not implying that you do this, occasionally overspend from their checking accounts. When this happens, the bank charges an NSF fee. The average fee for overspending from the checking account is $24 (national average). Some banks charge more. Some charge less.

Many people, furthermore, overspend more than once a year. The national average is between 3 and 4 times. This means that these people, and again I am not implying that you do this, pay between $72 and $96 every year, on a national average.

You can avoid this terrible wealth depleting habit if you build up some reserves at your bank.

To continue the example of my own banking strategy, by maintaining a minimum balance of $1,500 in my savings account, and having any overdrafts covered by this balance, I can potentially avoid more disastrous fees. If I avoid just one NSF fee per year for a total of $35, and I include the other benefits of avoiding maintenance fees, the deposit of $1,500 into savings is saving me a total of $237 plus interest. This is equal to 15.8% annually.

So much for the Personal Finance gurus or experts that say savings accounts are a waste of money.

If you build your cash reserves to a level where you can open, or re-open as the case may be, a checking account at your bank that also includes a savings account with a large enough deposit to eliminate the monthly fees on these accounts, you will probably avoid the added misery of being charged for the occasional overspend, or NSF, fee because the balance in the savings account will be used to cover the overspend. (Whew! That was a long sentence.)

Depending on where you have a bank account, the strategy may look somewhat different. The strategy is the same: savings accounts can earn a real rate of return that rivals stock or mutual fund investments.

Important Note: If you overspend, you will need to bring the balance of the savings account up to the required level as before, but the bank will usually give you a short time to do so.

Are you going to continue to believe the so-called experts that tell you a savings account is a waste of time and money? I didn't think so.

Chapter 12
Strategies to Create Cash Reserves

"Okay," you tell me. "That's all fine and dandy, but I only have $50 left over every month. How am I going to create any cash reserves?"

Great question. I have great answers.

I promised you I would provide useful strategies. Here they are. These strategies have worked, time and time again, for people who have a small or short-term financial goal that they need to accomplish but have little left over every month. One or more of these should work for you.

Strategy #1:

If is, of course, up to you to determine how much is an appropriate amount to have in cash reserves. I simply offer insight and some useful and proven methods to accomplish this goal.

You are, I assume, a normal person who has purchased things in the past over the course of your life. Many of those things were once fun or useful to have but have gone unused or forgotten as the months and years have passed.

This strategy simply proposes that you sell these things because you don't use them anymore or they are taking up too much space in your garage. You could have a Yard Sale on the weekend if there are enough things to sell. Or, you could go online and sell them via Facebook Marketplace, or Craig's List, or even on Ebay.

The recommendation is to let go of what is unimportant. What you don't need anymore can be translated into what you need today.

If you have some unused power tools in the garage, for example, put these tools to good work. Sell them and put the money into a savings account.

Did you ever think that the $100 power drill could help you save $84 every year?

Strategy #2:

Find a side-hustle. This is just another way of saying "second job." This second job or side-hustle doesn't necessarily mean you'll be working 20 additional hours per week and it doesn't mean you will be working two jobs forever. There are many ways to earn a few hundred per month by working only a few hours per week.

Ideas:

1. Do you have unique skills that could be turned into a freelance opportunity?
2. There are businesses, such as FedEx and UPS, who hire temporary workers during the holidays? Look into this. The companies that deliver Christmas presents pay extremely well.
3. Could you learn a skill that would allow you to earn a side income but don't know where to start?
4. Can you work for a friend, or a relative, and keep your hours low?
5.

All it takes is some creativity. The biggest resource you will need is something that is already available to you. I know this sounds obvious, but could you open up your creativity to find a side income by simply opening up Google.com and start searching? If you search for "Make Money From Home," you will find hundreds of pages of information that detail dozens of different ways to make money from the comfort of your own home.

If this is too overwhelming, go to Youtube.com and type in the same terms on their search bar. You will find hundreds of videos that describe and detail all sorts of ways to make money from home. Most of these do not require an employer and can be done on your schedule.

Strategy #3:

This strategy may seem like I am contradicting myself from earlier explanations. Wait before you make this judgement. This is a case of "good" debt, not "bad" debt.

Many people have supportive families and in many of these families there are members who have done well for themselves financially. If you are in a family with someone, such as an uncle or aunt or even one of your parents, who has done well for themselves financially, you could propose to them that they loan you the amount you need to open the new checking and savings accounts.

Specifically, I am suggesting a short-term loan (less than one year) of the amount it would take to open the type of checking account described above. To illustrate, I am assuming that $500 would allow you to open this type of account that would save you $5 per month and the added misery of being charged an NSF fee.

If you explain to this family member the strategy you are trying to implement, the logic and the potential savings would be obvious to them. In fact, if they had created their own wealth in their lives, they would understand perfectly what you are trying to do and might increase their respect for you as a result.

This is only an option if you have someone in your family who could loan the money to you and would be open enough to consider supporting you in this strategy.

In the months that follow, you can offer to pay them with the amount you have left over each month. If you borrow $500 and have $50 left over each month, the loan (interest free) will be paid off in ten months.

Here is some homework for you and it is the easiest yet.

Take some time to work out a plan for yourself to create the recommended levels of cash reserves. You already understand two very good reasons to have an adequate level of cash reserves in place.

Work out a plan. Then, implement the plan.

Now, imagine that you have put together a cash flow statement (Part I) and you have eliminated all of your consumer debt (Part II) and, finally, you have put together three months' worth of expenses into cash reserves (Part III).

Do you see and feel how much stronger you are financially?

If so, I will jump the gun this time and shout "CONGRATULATIONS!!!!"

If you have done all of the tasks and you are up to date so far, then it is time to move forward into Part IV.

Get ready. Here is where it gets really interesting . . .

Disclaimer: Any financial advice, technique, or opportunity revealed in this series of books or anything pertaining to financial markets, in part or as a whole, is purely for informational purposes only. Any insight gained by the reader is similarly for informational purposes and the author of this manuscript does not take responsibility for how this information is used.

Part IV

Chapter 13

The Source of All Wealth

You have made great strides so far. Keep going. The next section is going to focus on something different than the first three. In Part I, you built a Cash Flow Statement and created a Budget. In Part II, you put together a plan to eliminate all of your consumer debt. In Part III, you started building your Cash Reserves.

Part IV is about focusing on the Source of All Wealth.

The first three parts of this book are focused on where your money goes. In Part IV, we are going to focus on where your money comes from - your income - and how to increase that income in order to create wealth for you and your family.

I understand that you may have trouble seeing the light at the end of the tunnel while you are completing the important steps in the first three parts of this book. If you have not done all of the work in those parts of the book, I recommend that you finish it before moving forward in this chapter.

You may, in the future, expand into the stock market to build wealth, or you may evolve into a real estate focused plan to build wealth, or into some other area. In each of these, you will reach a point where your income is no longer the driving force of wealth creation but you have to reach that point first. Before this happens, your income will be your greatest asset and the source of all the wealth you will eventually create.

If you have completed all the work in Part I, II, and III, you may feel you are ready to start investing and I would generally agree with you. However, most people overlook the most important investment that they will ever make and focus on real estate or the stock market instead. Before you do this, there is one more area that you will need to concentrate on.

For some time, our country's most successful investor, Warren Buffett, has promoted a singular idea that he believes is the first and most important investment everyone can make. He is, without question, someone each of us should listen to and draw upon for guidance.

Warren Buffett's No. 1 tip for success is "to invest in yourself."

Wise words. Investing in yourself means learning, exploring, and discovering those hidden or undiscovered talents each of us have possessed since birth. They can be the source of increased levels of wealth but only if we tap into the potential of those unique talents.

You may be a wiz at math. Or you may have a particular talent for writing. Or you may have a rare and incredibly important talent for being a parent (Yes. There are ways to make extra money as a parent). Whatever the particular talent you possess, if you are not working to develop this talent by developing the skills and gaining experience, you will be passing up the best source of wealth you have for you and your family.

Many people never realize they have a talent for something either because of missed opportunities, shallow guidance, or they grew up in an environment that placed no value on what was obviously just under the surface. Imagine your favorite entertainer was never exposed to singing, or music, or theater. Imagine that in their youth, the leaders and teachers and parents provided no encouragement in those areas. Imagine this young boy or girl growing up in a family or an environment that simply didn't recognize these hidden talents as possible or worthwhile to pursue.

The world would be less of a beautiful place from the absence of that boy or girl's talent. And the world is already a less beautiful place if you have not found those special and unique talents that you were born with. Only by investing in yourself - learning new skills, pursuing knowledge or a profession simply because you feel strongly about it - can you discover what makes you special.

I am here to tell you, no matter who you are, you have unique talents. You may not have found them yet but you possess them even so.

These undiscovered talents can translate into greater levels of income. There are two ways you can use these talents by either evolving in your current job or finding something on your own that draws out your unique talents (a side-hustle).

Here's an example: After many days of soul searching, you have come to the conclusion that your strongest talent is what makes you a great parent. There are others like you who have turned this innate talent into immense levels of wealth. Go to Google.com. Search for blogs about parenting. The oldest and best known of these blogs are written and created by men and women who make tens of thousands of dollars each month from their blog. Sometimes more.

By increasing your income this way, it becomes more important than just money. Finding those talents within you is often so satisfying as to be the reward itself.

Okay. You're happy where you are, you say. You make plenty of money, you say. You aren't in a position to chase after hidden talents you can't even see, you say.

That's fine. Discovering your talents is completely up to you. You may go through your entire life and never discover these vibrant, enthralling parts of who you are. You have the option to do this. You always have this option and can choose it for as long as you wish. However . . .

If this admission rubs you the wrong way, or just doesn't sit right in your mind, then you already suspect these talents exist. You can feel that you should be doing something better with your life, something more important, if only more important to you. You should develop whatever talents you possess. You should develop these talents into higher levels of income. And, you should start today.

Chapter 14

A Very Short Story

I am very happy that you have made it this far in the book. I didn't have access to a book like this when I was a young adult. I'm nearly 60 years old now as I write this. When I was 20 years old, the internet didn't exist (sounds weird, doesn't it?). Personal computers were only a hobbyist's toy. Having access to the Universe's knowledge base was a plot reserved for science fiction.

You and I have these resources at our fingertips today. No matter what your age at this very minute, you live at a time when great personal discovery is only a few clicks away.

I did have access to libraries, however. I want to tell you a very short story to demonstrate how much more I could have done, how much farther I could have taken it, and how a hidden talent could have possibly become a source of increased income and wealth for me.

In my last year of High School in Phoenix, Arizona, I would very often go to the central library in downtown Phoenix to complete my homework on a Saturday or Sunday. The library's study areas were quiet and encouraged concentration. I could finish my homework much faster there than if I stayed at home.

Often, however, I would become distracted. I was only 17 years old so this was normal and expected.

One weekend, I became distracted again and needed a break. I began to casually look over books while taking a random walk through the peace and quiet of the library. I wasn't looking for anything in particular. I was just stepping away from my homework to clear my mind.

My eyes fell on a book and my hand casually pulled it from the shelf. It was a book on carpentry. Specifically, it was a book that detailed all the different techniques and methods of building a house. I had some interest in this as I had worked with wood before. As a young boy, a neighbor had helped me create a wooden skateboard in the woodshop behind his house. Woodshop in school, called "shop" to most of us, had also been something I liked and was something I was good at. I had worked on a construction site during the previous summer and had liked that too.

Inside the book I had pulled from the library shelf I found a chapter on building stairs in a house. I didn't know how to build stairs and while working construction the previous summer, I understood that it was a highly prized skill and a job for only the most experienced carpenters.

I read the chapter from beginning to end. I could see the planks of wood in my mind and the tools I would need and how to use them. I could see exactly how any form of stairs were built and imagined the entire process from start to finish. I can remember each step today as clearly as if I had just read that chapter again in the downtown library in Phoenix, Arizona.

In my early 20's, I found myself working for a furniture maker in southeast Phoenix. I had recently ended an enlistment in the US Army and had returned to finish college at Arizona State. I started helping out in this man's workshop and was soon getting paid to assist in furniture projects he was completing.

After a few months, he mentioned that he needed to make some changes in the shop and it would require building some stairs. He was surprised, and somewhat suspicious, when I said immediately that I knew how to make stairs. He waved me forward, explained where he needed a short flight of stairs constructed, and told me it was my project. He fully intended, I believed, to step in and correct what I was doing once he saw the mistakes I would probably make.

I had the stairs built in six hours. I had never built stairs before in my life but that book I pulled from the library shelf years before had shown me how. I had some talent for it, previously undiscovered, that made the diagrams in the book come to life.

I continued to learn in this man's workshop. I eventually took on projects by myself and completed cabinetry and various stand alone pieces of furniture. It was the most satisfying job I have ever had because I had discovered a unique talent for it. I have since had my own home remodeling company and have worked in Arizona, Florida, and California as a journeyman carpenter. All because I let one book, on an obscure shelf in a library, excite me and encourage what was waiting inside.

Imagine how far I might have taken this previously hidden talent if I had had access to the internet? Access that both of us have right now.

Chapter 15
The Skills You Need

There are two ways to go about increasing your income.

The first way is with your current employer. Just look at the employees who earn more money than you. What skills or experience do they have that you don't? How would you get those skills or experience that would qualify you for increased income?

Those higher paid employees may have easily acquired skills that you need:

1. The ability to speak to a small or large group of people and do so effectively.
2. The ability to write effectively and produce written forms of communication.
3. Training in management techniques that allow them to manage groups of people and projects that need groups of people.
4. Engineering experience. This may require you to begin college which is an expensive journey. There are, however, many excellent undergraduate programs in Engineering.
5. Tech skills that include coding, web design, or other technical experience. This area, surprisingly, does not require a college degree.

There are several excellent resources to learn new skills that can help you get promoted and increase your income. Go and investigate them and find a skill and a learning process that gets you excited:

1. Skilshare.com
2. Coursera.com
3. Udemy.com

4. Treehouse.com

The first one on this list is an online resource called Skilshare.com. For a low monthly subscription (I believe it is only $10), you can have access to hundreds, if not thousands, of skill building and instructional videos. This could be the "random walk down an obscure aisle in a downtown library" that will inspire and send you in a new direction.

Coursera.com is a wonderful skill building resource. There is a wide variety of courses including training in Human Resources, Accounting, and other business skills.

Udemy.com has probably the broadest selection of courses in video form. This may be the best place to start especially if you are leaning toward an entrepreneurial focus.

Treehouse.com is a specialized platform that focuses on high tech skills such as coding and web design. If you want to work in this field, this is the best resource out there.

The second way you can choose to increase your income is to work for yourself and create a side-hustle. This is something you learn to do from home by using the online resources that have been around for years. You can choose to spend all of your free time or just some of your free time pursuing a wide range of different opportunities.

This will, however, require you to be self-motivated. You will need to become an entrepreneur and perhaps this is the first skill to discover in yourself. Udemy.com and Skilshare.com are both great resources for entrepreneurs and for people to discover if they have what it takes to build a business for themselves.

I have some recommended areas for you to look into as you spend some time discovering on any of these four platforms. You may be encouraged by these opportunities or you may not like them at all. What you do with any of them is completely up to you. I am simply trying to provide a starting point for you. Where you take it depends on what you discover about you.

Side-hustle areas to consider.

Affiliate Marketing.

The fullest explanation of affiliate marketing is beyond the scope of this book. My suggestion is that you start exploring. A great resource for this is YouTube.com, and specifically, a YouTube channel called "Adam Enfroy". He does a terrific job going into detail and explaining the proven strategies for making money online. Look it up and see if it sparks something in you.

I highly recommend the YouTube Channel Adam Enfroy for his experience and willingness to reach out and help beginners. You can also discover great things on his website: milesbeckler.com

Write a book.

Publish it on Amazon.com's Kindle platform.

Here is where you can explore a talent you are only now discovering. Writing a book, just like I am doing right now, is not for everyone, however. Many people hate to write. I'm not one of them. I have discovered I have some talent for it. I finished college with a degree in English because I had discovered I love to write. I discovered such a huge desire to write that I eventually finished college at the University of California at Berkeley.

You might even discover you already have a story to tell. Remember the childrens' books about Harry Potter (no relation)? The author, J K Rowling, wrote the first book in that series while sitting in a cafe in London, England and often wrote sections of the story on paper napkins - the only thing available to write on, I assume. As the second or third wealthiest woman in Scotland, she certainly found one of her hidden talents and let it change her life.

There are wonderfully instructive videos on YouTube about writing and publishing on Amazon's Kindle platform. My recommendation is a channel called "Self Publishing with Dale". Check it out. This may be the beginning of a miraculous journey for you.

Create an Ecommerce business on Etsy or Shopify.

This is a proven ecommerce strategy and I will let you discover more for yourself on YouTube. Like the suggestions above, these side-hustles take some "hustle." You will have to discover if this is for you on your own. The good news is that there are plenty of resources for you to discover if you have hidden talents for ecommerce.

Tasked-Based Freelance Jobs.

This can be anything from transcribing audio files to conducting usability tests on websites. Use the Google search feature to discover more. "Transcription" or "Usability Testing" are great places to start your search.

No ideas yet? Go discover what may be the most important step you ever take in your life. This is about discovering what you already have inside you, your hidden talents, that may have gone unnoticed until now.

Join Skilshare.com if you are not sure what this could be right now. This is an inexpensive way to start. Or, take a casual "virtual" walk down the aisles on YouTube and embrace what excites you.

One last resource: we publish on our blog every week. Often we find a great resource for extra income and mention it there. A great reason to subscribe? Yes, it is.

There is homework. This time, it is different.

I want you to take an honest look at your work environment and your current employer. Do you believe there are opportunities for you to grow, to demonstrate new skills, and increase your income there?

If the answer is yes, this is where you should start. But, by no means, this is where it will end.

If the answer is no, you will need to look outside of your current job, and in the resources I've described, for ways to add to your current income or replace your current income altogether.

Until you take the step forward, you will never discover anything new. Until you step outside of what feels safe and comfortable, you will never grow.

The world is waiting for you to discover who you were born to be.

Disclaimer: Any financial advice, technique, or opportunity revealed in this series of books or anything pertaining to financial markets, in part or as a whole, is purely for informational purposes only. Any insight gained by the reader is similarly for informational purposes and the author of this manuscript does not take responsibility for how this information is used.

Conclusion

Chapter 16

This is the end. This is the beginning.

I've asked you to do great things in this book.

If you have followed through and taken the steps for yourself, you have accomplished truly great things. You are now ready to start implementing plans to create more wealth for yourself.

Yes! I did say "more" wealth.

When you created a Cash Flow Statement for yourself, you accomplished the first step. You created a wealth of knowledge about where your money goes. With this wealth of knowledge you can now begin to make fact-based decisions about where it goes in the future. This wealth will serve you as you go forward. It will be the basis of all the tangible and financial wealth you ever create for yourself from this moment on.

When you created a Budget, you created a valuable tool that will enable you to use the financial resources you already have right now to build the foundation for all wealth that will follow. Stick to this Budget as closely as you can. "Tighten your belt" as they say and use what remains at the end of the month to build this foundation into something indestructible.

The extra money you find at the end of the month, and hopefully it is more each month after reading this little book, is how you will turn the liabilities of debt into the assets of positive account balances. You may have several credit cards to overcome or you may have only one or none at all. Eliminating them for good, once and for all, removes this obstacle from your path. You are, by definition, wealthier when they are gone than you were before.

If you have removed all the debt then you can already see more extra money, your hard-earned dollars, at the end of the month. Build those Cash Reserves! Build them to a level that is appropriate for you.

Once you do this you will notice that one thing goes away and one thing remains.

Once you build your cash reserves, the burden of allocating your excess income to this foundation piece goes away. Once complete, you still have extra money at the end of the month and these dollars can then go towards building financial investments.

If you have taken my advice in Part IV and have begun developing your skills to rise up with your current employer, or built skills that can translate into productive side-hustles, I congratulate you on your courage. Not many people feel confident enough to take this step.

Keep going!! And understand something clearly as you begin. There will be times when it is difficult or frustrating and you don't know what to do next. Believe it or not, this is a great place to be. You are probably half a step away from a breakthrough. So, Keep Going !!!!

Thank you again for having the faith and desire to make it to these final pages. This book is not the end, however.

I finished writing this book in mid-February 2021. I will finish Book #2 in the summer of 2023. If you are one of the early readers and want to begin reading Book #2 when it is published, there is a simple way to go about it.

Much of what you have read here, but not all of it, is taken from our blog at tinbucketfinance.com. A great way for you to know when the next book becomes available is for you to subscribe to our blog. I will send you a summary of the new posts each week and when Book #2 is ready, I will notify you and offer a discount on the retail price.

Go to: tinbucketfinance.com

Subscribe and continue learning. For Free.

One more thing. On our website, you can contact me with questions or feedback on this book. I would very much like to hear from you. Just send me a message via email and I will respond in a day or so.

If we stay in contact, by email or as a subscriber, I will be looking for readers to review the next book in this series. I will disclose more details about this program as the books become available.

Thank you again. If you would like to leave a positive review of this book for other readers, please do so, but keep in mind that Amazon includes a rating form at the end of this book. These are two different kinds of reviews. I ask that you take the time to write a review on Amazon, instead of relying on the form at the end of this book. This kind of feedback goes a long way towards promoting this book and becoming available to new readers.

I wish you all the abundance that life has to offer,

George M. Potter

About the Author

George M Potter is a former financial advisor who worked for one of the largest financial services firms in the country, while prospering in Silicon Valley. The techniques and strategies discussed in the *Wealth Within Reach* series are based on years working with clients to help them reach their financial goals.

Even though he is retired from corporate life, he enjoys his life profoundly with his wife Robin and their five dogs in Montana.

Read more at https://tinbucketmedia.com.

www.ingramcontent.com/pod-product-compliance
Lightning Source LLC
LaVergne TN
LVHW090428210926
848480LV00002B/738